BRITISH
WARSHIPS
& AUXILIARIES

DAVID HANNAFORD

RMAS FAITHFUL trails HMS TORBAY as the "blue" submarine returns to Devonport.

THE ROYAL NAVY

What a good year 2006 has been. New aircraft carriers have been launched; large amphibious vessels, from flat-top LHDs to troop carrying LPDs have been accepted into service; nuclear-powered hunter-killer and modern AIP diesel powered submarines have been commissioned and the fleet of modern air defence destroyers is added to on an almost monthly basis. Innovative designs for warship classes to operate in coastal waters have been developed and are in build or entering service and new fleet replenishment tankers are ready to deploy. A good year, that is, if you are the United States, French, German, Japanese, Indian, Norwegian, Danish, Finnish or Spanish Navy. Anyone it would seem, other than the Royal Navy.

For some reason the RN's aspirations of becoming a modern, flexible expeditionary force, the cornerstone of the present government's defence policy for the past 10 years, is just not being delivered. For the Royal Navy, 2006 was another year without a major warship delivery. With much ceremony, the Offshore Patrol Vessel HMS CLYDE was named at Portsmouth and, as we went to press, was ready to be delivered to the RN - on lease. However, other than that, there has been nothing commissioned.

Everyone agrees that the RN of the Cold War needed to re-invent itself. For decades the RN had been designed for one purpose only. It was, in effect, a specialist ASW force, committed to NATO, in defence of the Northern Altantic choke points, should the super-powers of the day ever square up to one another. With the end of the Cold War, the "peace dividend" kicked in and the Treasury saw the opportunity for wholesale cuts to the whole of the Armed Forces. This was a grave mistake, and one from which we may never recover.

What the politicians failed to grasp was that the UK, no matter what the world situation, is, and always will be, an island nation. We rely on a steady trade of oil, gas, raw materials and food, 95% of which arrives by sea. This makes us vulnerable and we must have the ability to defend ourselves - an insurance policy, whose premium, in the grand scale of things, is a small price to pay. The days of relying on massive re-inforcements from across the pond if it all goes pear shaped are long gone. The UK must have a maritime force, strong enough to deter any aggressor. If a potential enemy can see no way of winning, he is unlikely to strike. Our insurance premium is worth paying.

Public perception of the RN is hard to judge, but I think they would be most surprised to hear of what a parlous state our maritime security is in. A member of the public enjoying a boat trip around Portsmouth may feel that the RN is in fine fettle - the advertising hoardings boast of 19 warships in port; 2 Assault Ships; 5 destroyers; 3 frigates; 6 minesweepers; a patrol boat; a depot ship and an aircraft carrier! How shocked would Joe Public be when he realises that all but one destroyer were in fact laid up awaiting disposal!

The public have read news reports of RN warships on the high seas successfully engaged in counter drug operations - four intercepts within two months in October and November 2006. They will have seen a veritable flotilla of ships going in and out of Beirut, as the RN was called upon to evacuate UK nationals from the war torn city. But again, this latter operation gave a flase impression - that the RN was able to mount this operation was down to pure luck. Those ships available were either returning from or going on deployment. Two weeks later the situation would have been very different. Public and to a large extent media "sea blindness' was dramatically demonstrated during this operation with public condemnation that the UK did not respond quickly enough and headlines condemning the fact that Italy and France were already evacuating their nationals, whilst the RN weren't even on the scene! Geography and distances involved in maritime operations did not seem to enter into their thought patterns - not to mention the maximum speed of ships like BULWARK.

There can be little doubt that the dramatically slimmed down RN is finding it hard to cope. It remains committed to supporting the wars in Afghanistan and Iraq; it still has committments to operations in the South Atlantic and Caribbean; it continues to operate in the Mediterranean in support of the Global War on Terror and it continues its security operations around the UK coastline. But, with fewer ships, the tempo of operations is unrelenting. As I write this (November 2006), I have just seen a press release, reporting that the frigate, LANCASTER, has deployed for operations off West Africa, South America and the Caribbean - only three months after returning from operations in the Gulf. This level of operations is hard on both crews and ships.

At the last round of defence cuts, the reasoning behind cutting six escorts was that revised maintenance schedules meant that operations could be conducted with fewer ships. How this pans out with the higher tempo of operations remains to be seen - working the remaining ships harder will surely result in a greater need for maintenance down time - another press release showed that HMS CHATHAM - has just clocked up 500,000 miles in 17 years of operation!

Studies are now underway to swap crews while destroyers and frigates are deployed, thereby keeping the ships on station longer. While this might negate the miles clocked up on lengthy transits to and from operational areas, it will result in a longer maintenance period on their return. And what of the individual ship's esprit de corps? Ships thrive on their reputations within the fleet - is such a reputation going to be garnered by a caretaker crew, who may only be aboard for four months? Will they still have that same feeling of pride? Will they still build up that affection which bonds both ship and crew?

The RN face ever increasing challenges as it struggles to match aspiration and budget. The operations in Iraq and Afghanistan, are, despite government protestations, seriously eating into the Equipment Plan budget. Ships have been laid up without repair or spares, to release money for frontline Army and RAF operations. Equipment being recycled from the frontline, is not being required immediately as funds are not available and new programmes are being delayed as budgets are getting squeezed.

The cornerstone of the governments expeditionary force restructuring has been the planned acquisition of two aircraft carriers for the Royal Navy. 2007 will see the 10th anniversay since that requirement was first issued. Ten years in which no order has been forthcoming. Main Gate submission, where budget approval would clear the way for contracts to be issued, was supposed to be In October. As we went to press in late November there had still been no official announcment. These 65,000 ton carriers are essential to the regeneration of both the RN and the forces they will ultimately support. Originally to have been in service in 2012, the government have now given up on predicting an in service date. The French are now onboard this project too, with a requirement for a single carrier, but while they press ahead with a conventional cat and trap design, the UK insist on a ski jump and the technically risky and unecessary Vertical/Short Take-Off version of the Joint Strike Fighter. Already deferred by the US the UK will have to buy from the Low Rate Initial Production batch if they wish to meet a 2014 in service date. These aircraft will be far more expensive to acquire and less capable than the Block III production aircraft. Already the initial buy of up to 150 aircraft has been cut to up to 138 aircraft. It remains a mystery as to why anyone would want to buy a compromised aircraft when there is a fully carrier operable design available - less technical risk, greater range, greater payload and with a 65,000 ton carrier there would be plenty of room to operate, not only that aircraft, but any carrier aircraft from both the French and US Navies.

The Type 45 destroyer programme is likely to deliver its first ship by the time the next volume of *British Warships* is published in 2008. But again the long term future of this programme is in doubt. The first three vessels are being built and the hulls of the second three have been contracted for, but there are still, reportedly, wranglings going on between the MoD and BAE. The manufacturer is demanding more money for modifications requested by MoD - the "cost" of these extras, being the sticking point. But where does this leave the programme? Are future ships going to be ordered? This class was once - a few years ago - going to be *'up to' 12 ships.* Subsequently cut to just eight, the signs are that it might not proceed beyond six. With potentially two 65,000 ton aircraft carriers and three large amphibious ships which will require some form of air cover on operations, it is hard to see how even eight air defence ships can fulfil the role.

It is a similar story with the Astute class submarines. Although the programme is back on track after a major restructuring, the boats will be late entering service, and there seems very little urgency to order anymore than the three presently under construction, despite the protestations of BAE that it will need orders if it is to retain this specialist workforce.

And this, perhaps, is the crux of the matter. There is a determination within government, it would appear, to stall, or slow down major projects - thereby delaying the point at which massive funding has to be committed. As the government itself is the architect for this re-equipment programme the only reason for delay can be the lack of funding.

A recent paper by the Royal United Services Institute (RUSI) has stated, that not only are *"the Armed Forces underfunded by between £10 - 15 billion"*, but that *"instead of the £2Bn saving in acquisition costs promised by the SDR, we are now at the stage where MoD needs a budget increase of around 30% a year just to maintain investment in current programmes"*.

Despite constant government claims that defence spending has risen year on year, they need to look at the cost of current operations, and the staggering costs of procurement projects to show that the percentage of money available to the frontline forces is decreasing "year on year" at an alarming rate.

The much vaunted "smart procurement" system is not working. The Defence Industrial Strategy is supposed to be addressing this and of significance to the RN, the Maritime Strategy, should allow for greater competition, better pricing and iron out some of the "feast to famine" scenarios associated with naval ship production. Without doubt there is over capacity in the Naval shipbuilding and refitting market within the UK. As the fleet has shrunk so rapidly over the past decade, the infrastructure has not. There seems little doubt that naval shipbuilding orders in the UK will ever again be of a magnitude to be able to support the present industry. There can, equally be little doubt that the RN of today hardly needs the base port facilities currently maintained. The latest surface ship refit contracts have been shared out equally between Rosyth, Devonport and Portsmouth - not the best way of guaranteeing value for money. There is a Base review underway and it is scheduled to report in Spring 2007. There will have to be cuts, but where the hatchet falls remains to be seen. If the Maritime Strategy can deliver a "cradle to grave" approach for ship acquisition and maintenance, then cuts to the Naval Bases could be greater than anticipated.

And what of the fleet itself? Have we seen the end of the savage cuts which have been a regular feature since SDR? I regret not. With the budget under such strain and no sign of a solution to the Iraq or Afghanistan problems, savings will be necessary - and the quickest way to make savings is to cut operational overheads. This government's track record in creating capability gaps, while awaiting new equipment sets a worrying precedent. But what will be in the firing line for a future reduction in numbers?

Despite being placed in reserve "until 2010" it is likely that early in 2007 INVINCIBLE will be put up for disposal. There are few who believe that she will ever return to service under the White Ensign. The Type 42 Batch II destroyers are very long in the tooth and expensive to maintain. With the first of the Daring class being delivered in 2008 it is not beyond the realms of possibility that a couple of Type 42's may creep into Extended Readiness, never to sail again (but nominally still credited as a fleet asset). Either ALBION or BULWARK could be laid up, just one LPD operating, as with the earlier FEARLESS and INTREPID - and with the introduction of the very capable Bay class LSD(A)s the pain would not be that great. With ARK

ROYAL operating in the LPH role it is not beyond the realms of possibility that OCEAN could find herself in a period of ER prior to her much needed refit. Frigate numbers are hard to cut. The Type 22, although the oldest, provide a unique capability and are unlikley to go, but there are signs that some Type 23s might go into ER - those not being upgraded with the new sonar for example. Controversial and soon to be debated, is the Nuclear Deterrant - Do we still need such a complex and expensive system as Trident? Would a modified Astute with fewer missiles, still represent a credible, but more affordable, system when considering potential enemies in the 21st century? If Trident is to be replaced it is going to be a financial strain on an already hard pressed RN budget. And finally, could there not be a cheaper solution of providing sea experience for university students, other than an expensive to operate squadron of fair weather only patrol vessels? Whatever the decision, the outcome will remain the same - there will be no new money from the Treasury. The MoD will have to generate cash from within the department - and that means cuts.

As 2007 runs its course, talk will inevitably change to the following year's general election. Prime topics for debate will be Social Security, Health and Education; Immigration policy and finally, after Green and Eco issues have been debated - Defence - but only in as much as the wars in Iraq and Afghanistan are concerned. Homeland Security will be a buzz phrase during any election campaign. My guess is that very few will realise that strong Homeland Security starts with secure borders and that for an island nation such security requires a strong patrol presence around our shores - the traditional domain of the RN, if only it had the tools for the job.

Will the Labour government and SDR remain and will the aircraft carriers and Type 45 destroyers ever see the light of day? (I am reminded that it was forty years ago that the last fixed wing carrier project was cancelled - by a Labour government). Or will the Conservative Party occupy No 10 and the whole process of reviews and reshaping start again? One thing is certain. There will be no great talk of increased defence spending - there is simply no money to go around. Funding the defence of the nation it seems is not as important as pandering to the demands of the growing and very vocal lobby of Eco-warriors. Something I can ponder whilst I am stuck in the roadworks on my way home as yet another three miles of cycle lane are installed!

Steve Bush
November 2006

SHIPS OF THE ROYAL NAVY
Pennant Numbers

Ship	Pennant Number	Page	Ship	Pennant Number	Page
Aircraft Carriers			IRON DUKE	F234	18
			MONMOUTH	F235	18
INVINCIBLE	R05	13	MONTROSE	F236	18
ILLUSTRIOUS	R06	13	WESTMINSTER	F237	18
ARK ROYAL	R07	13	NORTHUMBERLAND	F238	18
			RICHMOND	F239	18
Assault Ships					
			Submarines		
OCEAN	L12	14			
ALBION	L14	15	VANGUARD	S28	10
BULWARK	L15	15	VICTORIOUS	S29	10
			VIGILANT	S30	10
Destroyers			VENGEANCE	S31	10
			TURBULENT	S87	11
EXETER	D89	16	TIRELESS	S88	11
SOUTHAMPTON	D90	16	TORBAY	S90	11
NOTTINGHAM	D91	16	TRENCHANT	S91	11
LIVERPOOL	D92	16	TALENT	S92	11
MANCHESTER	D95	17	TRIUMPH	S93	11
GLOUCESTER	D96	17	SCEPTRE	S104	12
EDINBURGH	D97	17	TRAFALGAR	S107	11
YORK	D98	17	SUPERB	S109	12
Frigates			**Minehunters**		
KENT	F78	18	LEDBURY	M30	21
PORTLAND	F79	18	CATTISTOCK	M31	21
SUTHERLAND	F81	18	BROCKLESBY	M33	21
SOMERSET	F82	18	MIDDLETON	M34	21
ST ALBANS	F83	18	CHIDDINGFOLD	M37	21
CUMBERLAND	F85	20	ATHERSTONE	M38	21
CAMPBELTOWN	F86	20	HURWORTH	M39	21
CHATHAM	F87	20	QUORN	M41	21
CORNWALL	F99	20	WALNEY	M104	22
LANCASTER	F229	18	PENZANCE	M106	22
ARGYLL	F231	18	PEMBROKE	M107	22

Ship	Pennant Number	Page	Ship	Pennant Number	Page
GRIMSBY	M108	22	DASHER	P280	26
BANGOR	M109	22	TYNE	P281	23
RAMSEY	M110	22	SEVERN	P282	23
BLYTH	M111	22	MERSEY	P283	23
SHOREHAM	M112	22	SCIMITAR	P284	25
			SABRE	P285	25
Patrol Craft			PUNCHER	P291	26
			CHARGER	P292	26
			RANGER	P293	26
EXPRESS	P163	26	TRUMPETER	P294	26
EXPLORER	P164	26			
EXAMPLE	P165	26	**Survey Ships & RN Manned Auxiliaries**		
EXPLOIT	P167	26			
CLYDE	P257	24			
ARCHER	P264	26	GLEANER	H86	31
BITER	P270	26	ECHO	H87	29
SMITER	P272	26	ENTERPRISE	H88	29
PURSUER	P273	26	ROEBUCK	H130	30
TRACKER	P274	26	SCOTT	H131	28
RAIDER	P275	26	ENDURANCE	A171	32
BLAZER	P279	26			

US NAVY WARSHIPS AND AUXILIARIES

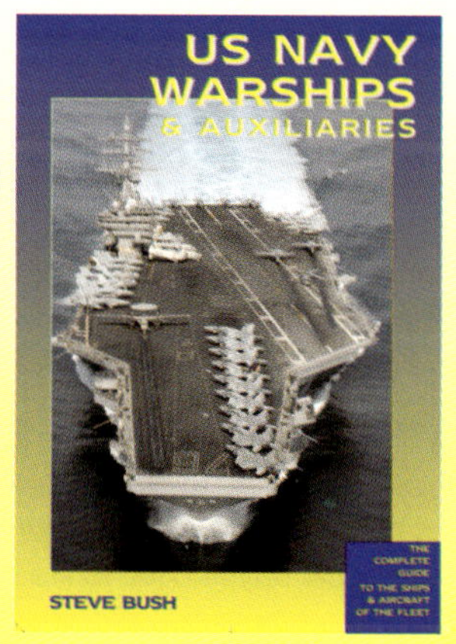

For the first time in a handy pocket sized reference book. Catch up with the ships, submarines and aircraft of the US Navy, Military Sealift Command and Ready Reserve Fleet. This up-to-date guide has entries for all current and future ships in build. In full colour packed with facts and over 100 photos. 168 pages.

£9.99 (inc UK post)

VANGUARD CLASS

Ship	Pennant Number	Completion Date	Builder
VANGUARD	S28	1992	VSEL
VICTORIOUS	S29	1994	VSEL
VIGILANT	S30	1997	VSEL
VENGEANCE	S31	1999	VSEL

Displacement 15,000 tons (dived) **Dimensions** 150m x 13m x 12m **Speed** 25 + dived
Armament 16 - Trident 2 (D5) missiles, 4 Torpedo Tubes **Complement** 132

Notes

After the first successful UK D5 missile firing in May '94 the first operational patrol was carried out in early '95 and a patrol has been constantly maintained ever since. According to a parliamentary answer in 2005 the UK's Trident missiles have been de-targeted since 1994, and the submarine on deterrent patrol is normally at several days notice to fire her missiles. The submarines have two crews each to maintain the maximum period on patrol. VICTORIOUS entered refit in 2005 and is scheduled to return to service in 2008.

TRAFALGAR CLASS

Ship	Pennant Number	Completion Date	Builder
TURBULENT	S87	1984	Vickers
TIRELESS	S88	1985	Vickers
TORBAY	S90	1986	Vickers
TRENCHANT	S91	1989	Vickers
TALENT	S92	1990	Vickers
TRIUMPH	S93	1991	Vickers
TRAFALGAR	S107	1983	Vickers

Displacement 4,500 tons **Dimensions** 85m x 10m x 8m **Speed** 30+ dived **Armament** 5 Torpedo Tubes; Tomahawk cruise missiles **Complement** 110.

Notes

Quieter, faster and with greater endurance than the Swiftsure class. Tomahawk Cruise Missiles are fitted in TRIUMPH, TRAFALGAR, TURBULENT and TRENCHANT. It is expected Tomahawk will eventually be fitted in all of these boats by the end of 2007. TORBAY is trialling a blue colour scheme on the hull. Decommissioning dates announced by the MoD remain: TRAFALGAR (2008); TURBULENT (2009); TIRELESS (2011); TALENT (2017), TRIUMPH (2019); TORBAY (2021) and TRENCHANT (2023).

SWIFTSURE CLASS

Ship	Pennant Number	Completion Date	Builder
SCEPTRE	S104	1978	Vickers
SUPERB	S109	1976	Vickers

Displacement 4,500 tons dived **Dimensions** 83m x 10m x 8m **Speed** 30 knots + dived **Armament** 5 Torpedo Tubes **Complement** 116.

Notes

Only two of the original class of six remain in service and both are based at Faslane. Decommissioning dates announced by the MoD are now:- SUPERB (2008) and SCEP-TRE (2010). Both SPARTAN and SOVEREIGN decommissioned in 2006. Both are at Devonport awaiting defuelling and storage afloat.

• DAVE CULLEN   **HMS Ark Royal**

INVINCIBLE CLASS

Ship	Pennant Number	Completion Date	Builder
INVINCIBLE	R05	1979	Vickers
ILLUSTRIOUS	R06	1982	Swan Hunter
ARK ROYAL	R07	1985	Swan Hunter

Displacement 22,500 tonnes **Dimensions** 210m x 36m x 6.5m **Speed** 28 knots **Armament** 2 - 20mm guns, 3 Phalanx/Goalkeeper **Aircraft** Tailored Air Group (Harrier GR9, Merlin, Sea King, Chinook as required) **Complement** 752 + 384 Air Group (600 troops in LPH role).

Notes

Only one carrier operational at any one time. ILLUSTRIOUS assumed the role of fleet flagship in June 2005. ARK ROYAL completed a refit at Rosyth at the end of 2006 where she received a mizzen mast at the end of the island structure and was converted to operate in both the Strike Carrier or LPH role. She will operate as an LPH to cover for OCEAN when she enters refit. INVINCIBLE decommissioned in July 2005 and was placed at Extended Readiness at Portsmouth until 2010 when she is likely to be put up for disposal. Vessels are now roled as Strike Carriers rather than ASW vessels and as such deploy with a Tailored Air Group to meet the specific operational needs of any deployment.

HMS Ocean

LANDING PLATFORM HELICOPTER (LPH)

Ship	Pennant Number	Completion Date	Builder
OCEAN	L12	1998	Kvaerner

Displacement 21,578 tonnes **Dimensions** 208m x 34m x 6.6m **Speed** 17 knots **Armament** 3 x Phalanx, 6 x 30mm BMARC guns **Complement** Ship 284, Squadrons 180, Embarked force 800.

Notes

Can carry 12 Sea King and 6 Lynx helicopters. Frequently employed as the flagship of the UK Amphibious Ready Group. RAF Chinook helicopters are normally carried as an integral part of the ship's air group, but they are unable to be stowed below decks. During a docking period at the end of 2002 she was modified with two 50m blisters attached to the hull at the waterline below the after chine to improve safety margins while deploying LCVPs from the after davits. Vessel is somewhat con-strained by her slow speed. Scheduled to refit in 2007 and be replaced by ARK ROYAL.

LANDING PLATFORM DOCK (LPD)

ALBION CLASS

Ship	Pennant Number	Completion Date	Builder
ALBION	L14	2003	BAE Systems
BULWARK	L15	2004	BAE Systems

Displacement 18,500 tons, 21,500 tons (flooded) **Dimensions** 176m x 25.6m x 6.1m
Speed 18 knots **Armament** 2 x CIWS, 2 x 20mm guns (single) **Complement** 325
Military Lift 303 troops, with an overload capacity of a further 405.

Notes

Vehicle deck capacity for up to six Challenger 2 tanks or around 30 armoured all-terrain
tracked vehicles. Floodable well dock, with the capacity to take four utility landing craft. Four
smaller landing craft on davits, each capable of carrying 35 troops each. Two-spot flight
deck able to take medium support helicopters and stow a third. The Flight Deck is capable
of taking the Chinook. These vessels do not have a hangar but have equipment needed
to support aircraft operations. Diesel/electric propulsion.

HMS Southampton

DESTROYERS
SHEFFIELD CLASS
(Type 42) Batch 2

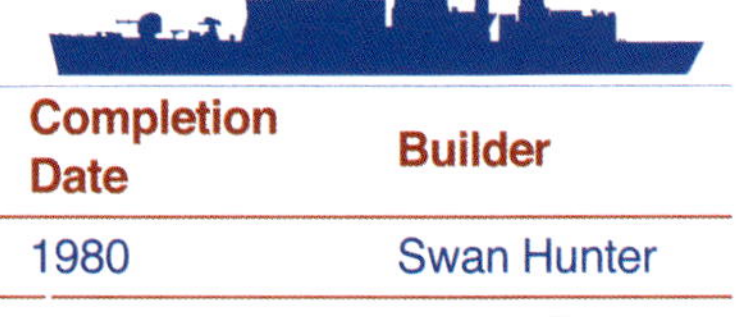

Ship	Pennant Number	Completion Date	Builder
EXETER	D89	1980	Swan Hunter
SOUTHAMPTON	D90	1981	Vosper T.
NOTTINGHAM	D91	1982	Vosper T.
LIVERPOOL	D92	1982	C. Laird

Displacement 3,660 tons **Dimensions** 125m x 15m x 7m **Speed** 29 knots **Armament** 1 - 4.5-inch gun, 4 - 20mm guns, Sea Dart Missile System: 2 - Phalanx, Lynx Helicopter, 6 Torpedo Tubes **Complement** 266.

Notes

The following decommissioning dates announced by the MoD remain: LIVERPOOL (2009); EXETER (2009); SOUTHAMPTON (2010) and NOTTINGHAM (2012). It is expected that the ships will be paid off as each Type 45 destroyer enters service. The first of these, DARING, has a scheduled In Service Date of 2009.

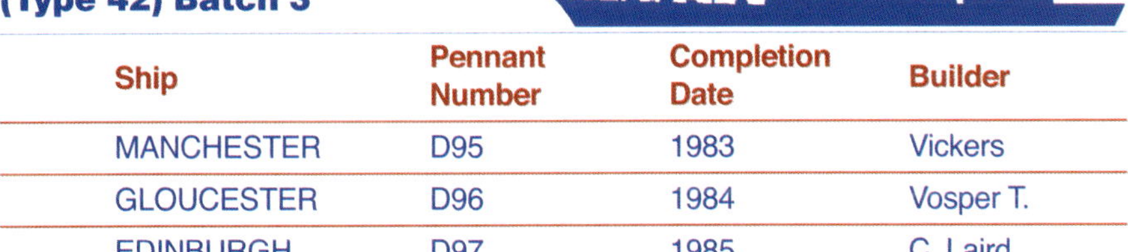

• MIKE WELSFORD   **HMS Edinburgh**

SHEFFIELD CLASS
(Type 42) Batch 3

Ship	Pennant Number	Completion Date	Builder
MANCHESTER	D95	1983	Vickers
GLOUCESTER	D96	1984	Vosper T.
EDINBURGH	D97	1985	C. Laird
YORK	D98	1984	Swan Hunter

Displacement 4,775 tons **Dimensions** 132m x 15m x 7m **Speed** 30 knots + **Armament** 1- 4.5-inch gun, 2 - Phalanx, 2 - 20mm guns, Sea Dart missile system, Lynx Helicopter, 6 Torpedo Tubes **Complement** 269.

Notes
Stretched versions of earlier ships of this class. Designed to provide area defence of a task force. Deck edge stiffening fitted to counter increased hull stress. EDINBURGH and YORK (only) fitted with 4.5-inch Mod 1 gun. The following decommissioning dates remain: MANCHESTER & GLOUCESTER (2011), YORK (2012) & EDINBURGH (2013). Vessels are now frequently seen without the distinctive radome covers over their Type 909 trackers. MANCHESTER returned to service in 2006 following a refit during which she was fitted with a stern flap for increased hydro-dynamic efficiency and fuel economy.

FRIGATES

DUKE CLASS (Type 23)

Ship	Pennant Number	Completion Date	Builder
KENT	F78	2000	Yarrow
PORTLAND	F79	2000	Yarrow
SUTHERLAND	F81	1997	Yarrow
SOMERSET	F82	1996	Yarrow
ST ALBANS	F83	2001	Yarrow
LANCASTER*	F229	1991	Yarrow
ARGYLL	F231	1991	Yarrow
IRON DUKE*	F234	1992	Yarrow
MONMOUTH*	F235	1993	Yarrow
MONTROSE*	F236	1993	Yarrow
WESTMINSTER	F237	1993	Swan Hunter
NORTHUMBERLAND*	F238	1994	Swan Hunter
RICHMOND	F239	1994	Swan Hunter

Displacement 3,500 tons **Dimensions** 133m x 15m x 5m **Speed** 28 knots **Armament** Harpoon & Seawolf missile systems: 1 - 4.5-inch gun, 2 - single 30mm guns, 4 - 2 twin, magazine launched, Torpedo Tubes, Lynx or Merlin helicopter **Complement** 173.

Notes

The ships incorporate 'Stealth' technology to minimise magnetic, radar, acoustic and infra-red signatures. Gas turbine and diesel electric propulsion. Those ships marked * have been fitted with the Mk 8 Mod 1 4.5-inch gun. The rest of class to be fitted by 2011. Type 2087 Sonar is to be fitted in only 9 of the remaining 13 of the class (ARGYLL, MONTROSE, MONMOUTH and IRON DUKE will not receive the upgrade).

The former NORFOLK, MARLBOROUGH and GRAFTON are undergoing regeneration at Portsmouth prior to transfer to the Chilean Navy. To be named ALMIRANTE COCHRANE, ALMIRANTE LYNCH and ALMIRANTE CONDELL respectively, they are to be delivered in 2007/08.

F238

• MIKE WELSFORD   **HMS Campbeltown**

BROADSWORD CLASS
(Type 22) Batch 3

Ship	Pennant Number	Completion Date	Builder
CUMBERLAND	F85	1988	Yarrow
CAMPBELTOWN	F86	1988	C. Laird
CHATHAM	F87	1989	Swan Hunter
CORNWALL	F99	1987	Yarrow

Displacement 4,200 tons **Dimensions** 147m x 15m x 7m **Speed** 30 knots **Armament** 1 - 4.5-inch gun, 1 - Goalkeeper, 8 - Harpoon, 2 - Seawolf, 2 - 20mm guns, 6 Torpedo Tubes, 2 Lynx or 1 Sea King Helicopter **Complement** 259.

Notes

All these ships have an anti-submarine and intelligence gathering capability. All are capable of acting as fleet flagships. CUMBERLAND fitted with Mk8 4.5-inch Mod 1 gun in 2001 and the remainder will be fitted by the end of the decade.

• CHRIS ROGERS   **HMS Quorn**

MINE COUNTERMEASURES SHIPS (MCMV'S) HUNT CLASS

Ship	Pennant Number	Completion Date	Builder
LEDBURY	M30	1981	Vosper T.
CATTISTOCK	M31	1982	Vosper T.
BROCKLESBY	M33	1983	Vosper T.
MIDDLETON	M34	1984	Yarrow
CHIDDINGFOLD	M37	1984	Vosper T.
ATHERSTONE	M38	1987	Vosper T.
HURWORTH	M39	1985	Vosper T.
QUORN	M41	1989	Vosper T.

Displacement 625 tonnes **Dimensions** 60m x 10m x 2.2m **Speed** 17 knots **Armament** 1 x 30mm + 2 x 20mm guns **Complement** 42.

Notes

The largest warships ever built of glass reinforced plastic. Their cost (£35m each) has dictated the size of the class. Very sophisticated ships - and lively seaboats! All are based at Portsmouth. Ships are frequently deployed in the Fishery Protection role. BROCK-LESBY, CHIDDINGFOLD, QUORN, HURWORTH and ATHERSTONE are scheduled to decommission in 2020 and LEDBURY in 2023. BRECON, which was with drawn from service in 2004, is likely to find a new role as a static Seamanship Training Vessel attached to the New Entry Training Establishment, HMS RALEIGH, at Torpoint.

• DOUGLAS S. COULL   **HMS Penzance**

SANDOWN CLASS

Ship	Pennant Number	Completion Date	Builder
WALNEY	M104	1992	Vosper T.
PENZANCE	M106	1998	Vosper T.
PEMBROKE	M107	1998	Vosper T.
GRIMSBY	M108	1999	Vosper T.
BANGOR	M109	2000	Vosper T.
RAMSEY	M110	2000	Vosper T.
BLYTH	M111	2001	Vosper T.
SHOREHAM	M112	2001	Vosper T.

Displacement 450 tons **Dimensions** 53m x 10m x 2m **Speed** 13 knots **Armament** 1 - 30mm gun **Complement** 34.

Notes

A class dedicated to a single mine hunting role. Propulsion is by vectored thrust and bow thrusters. All are based at Faslane. In October 2006 BLYTH and RAMSEY sailed from Faslane for an extended two year deployment to the Gulf. CROMER paid off in 2001 and was towed to Dartmouth in 2002 to become a static training hull (renamed HINDUSTAN). BRIDPORT, SANDOWN and INVERNESS, all paid off in 2005 as a defence economy, are undergoing regeneration prior to transfer to the Estonian Navy.

• CHRIS ROGERS

HMS Mersey

PATROL VESSELS

RIVER CLASS

Ship	Pennant Number	Completion Date	Builder
TYNE	P281	2002	Vosper T.
SEVERN	P282	2003	Vosper T.
MERSEY	P283	2003	Vosper T.

Displacement 1700 tonnes **Dimensions** 80m x 13.5m x 3.8m **Speed** 20+ knots
Armament 1 x 20mm, 2 x GPMG **Complement** 48

Notes

Ordered on 8 May 2001, the deal is unusual in that the ships are being leased from
Vospers (VT) for five years under a £60 million contract. Thereafter the opportunity
exists for the lease to be extended, the ships purchased outright or returned to VT. So
far the arrangement seems to have been a success with VT meeting their commitment
of having the ships available for over 300 days a year.

BATCH II RIVER CLASS

Ship	Pennant Number	Completion Date	Builder
CLYDE	P257	2006	VT Shipbuilding

Displacement 1,850 tons **Dimensions** 81.5m x 13.6m x 3.8m **Speed** 19 knots (full load) 21 knots (sprint) **Aircraft** Flight Deck to take Lynx, Sea King or Merlin Helicopter **Armament** 1 - 30mm gun **Complement** 36 (space for additional 20 personnel)

Notes

Designed to carry out patrol duties around the Falklands and their dependencies, the ship is able to accommodate a single helicopter up to Merlin size. CLYDE was launched from Vosper Thornycroft's Portsmouth facility on 20 June 2006 and accepted into service on 31 October. She is expected to deploy to the Falklands for the first time in May 2007. It is envisaged that CLYDE's more modern design will enable her to remain on task in the South Atlantic until 2012. Like the previous River class, she has been leased from the VT Group, for a period of five years.

CLYDE will replace the two Castle class ships. LEEDS CASTLE paid off in August 2005 and DUMBARTON CASTLE in 2007. Both are reported to have been acquired by Bangladesh.

• DARRELL KING HMS Sabre

LIFESPAN PATROL VESSELS (LPVs)

Ship	Pennant Number	Completion Date	Builder
SCIMITAR	P284	1988	Halmatic
SABRE	P285	1988	Halmatic

Displacement 18.5 tons   **Dimensions** 16m x 4.7m x 1.4m   **Speed** 27+ knots
Armament 2 x GPMG   **Complement** 4

Notes

Purpose built in 1988 for counter terrorism duties on Lough Neagh, Northern Ireland. Operated in anonimity until withdrawn from service in 2002, following a review of RN operations in the Province. Transferred to Gibraltar in September 2002 to join the Gibraltar Patrol Boat Squadron. On completion of trials they were commissioned on 31 January 2003 and renamed SCIMITAR (ex-GREYFOX) and SABRE (ex-GREY-WOLF). They replaced the P2000 patrol boats TRUMPETER and RANGER at Gibraltar.

COASTAL TRAINING CRAFT
P2000 CLASS

Ship	Pennant Number	Completion Date	Builder
EXPRESS	P163	1988	Vosper T.
EXPLORER	P164	1985	Watercraft
EXAMPLE	P165	1985	Watercraft
EXPLOIT	P167	1988	Vosper T.
ARCHER	P264	1985	Watercraft
BITER	P270	1985	Watercraft
SMITER	P272	1986	Watercraft
PURSUER	P273	1988	Vosper T.
TRACKER	P274	1998	Ailsa Troon
RAIDER	P275	1998	Ailsa Troon
BLAZER	P279	1988	Vosper T.
DASHER	P280	1988	Vosper T.
PUNCHER	P291	1988	Vosper T.
CHARGER	P292	1988	Vosper T.
RANGER	P293	1988	Vosper T.
TRUMPETER	P294	1988	Vosper T.

Displacement 43 tonnes **Dimensions** 20m x 6m x 1m **Speed** 20 knots **Armament** 1 x GPMG (Cyprus based vessels) **Complement** 5 (with accommodation for up to 12 under-graduates).

Notes

In service with RN University units (URNU) as training vessels. TRUMPETER and RANGER deployed to Gibraltar in 1991 and armed in 2002. TRUMPETER returned to the UK in 2003 and RANGER followed in 2004. DASHER and PURSUER were transferred to Cyprus at the end of 2002 to form a new Cyprus Squadron to patrol off the Sovereign Base Areas. Remaining vessels are assigned to the following URNUs: ARCHER (Aberdeen); BITER (Manchester); BLAZER (Southampton); CHARGER (Liverpool); TRUMPETER (Bristol); EXAMPLE (Northumbria); EXPLOIT (Birmingham); EXPLORER (Yorkshire); EXPRESS (Wales); PUNCHER (London); RANGER (Sussex); RAIDER (Cambridge); SMITER (Glasgow); TRACKER (Oxford).

• MICHAEL NITZ - NAVAL PRESS SERVICE

HMS Explorer

•CHRIS ROGERS

HMS Exploit

• DAVID HANNAFORD

HMS Scott

SURVEY SHIPS

Ship	Pennant Number	Completion Date	Builder
SCOTT	H 131	1997	Appledore

Displacement 13,300 tonnes **Dimensions** 131.5m x 21.5m x 9m **Speed** 17 knots **Complement** 63

Notes

SCOTT carries a mixture of the latest UK and US survey equipment. The sonar system is US supplied. She operates a three watch system whereby the vessel is run by 42 of her ships company of 63 - with the remainder on leave. Each crew member works 75 days in the ship before having 30 days off, allowing her to spend more than 300 days at sea in a year. These manpower reductions over previous survey ships have been possible because of the extensive use of commercial lean manning methods including unmanned machinery spaces, fixed fire fighting systems and extensive machinery and safety surveillance technology.

• DAVE CULLEN

HMS Echo

ECHO CLASS

Ship	Pennant Number	Completion Date	Builder
ECHO	H 87	2002	Appledore
ENTERPRISE	H 88	2003	Appledore

Displacement 3,470 tonnes **Dimensions** 90m x 16.8m x 5.5.m **Speed** 15 knots **Armament** 1 x 20mm **Complement** 46 (with accommodation for 81)

Notes

In June 2000, a £130 million order was placed with prime contractor Vosper Thornycroft to build and maintain, over a 25 year period, these two new Survey Vessels Hydrographic Oceanographic (SVHO). Both vessels were built by sub-contractor Appledore Shipbuilding Limited. They have a secondary role as mine countermeasures flag ships. ECHO entered service in 2003 and ENTERPRISE followed in 2004. They will be operationally available for 330 days a year. Utilizing a diesel electric propulsion system, they have three main generators. They are the first RN ships to be fitted with Azimuth pod thrusters in place of the more normal shaft and propellor. Each ship carries a namod survey launch, PATHFINDER (ECHO) and PIONEER (ENTERPRISE).

• MIKE WELSFORD

HMS Roebuck

COASTAL SURVEY VESSEL

Ship	Pennant Number	Completion Date	Builder
ROEBUCK	H130	1986	Brooke Marine

Displacement 1500 tonnes **Dimensions** 64m x 13m x 4m **Speed** 15 knots
Armament 1 x 20mm; Mk 44 Mini-guns **Complement** 51.

Notes

Able to operate for long periods away from shore support, this ship and the other vessels of the Hydrographic Fleet collect the data that is required to produce the Admiralty Charts and publications which are sold to mariners worldwide. Fitted with the latest fixing aids and sector scanning sonar. Emerged from a refit at Devonport in 2005 which will allow the ship to serve until 2014. Upgrades have included a new armament to complement the emerging frontline operational role for the survey squadron.

• WALTER SARTORI

HMS Gleaner

INSHORE SURVEY VESSEL

Ship	Pennant Number	Completion Date	Builder
GLEANER	H86	1983	Emsworth

Displacement 22 tons **Dimensions** 14.8m x 4.7m x 1.3m **Speed** 14 knots **Complement** 5.

Notes
Small inshore survey craft used for the collection of data from the shallowest inshore waters. Its future beyond 2007 is unknown.

• MIKE WELSFORD

HMS Endurance

ICE PATROL SHIP

Ship	Pennant Number	Completion Date	Builder
ENDURANCE	A171	1990	Ulstein-Hatlo

Displacement 5,129 tons **Dimensions** 91m x 17.9m x 6.5m **Speed** 14.9 knots
Armament Small arms **Aircraft** 2 Lynx **Complement** 116

Notes

Chartered for only 7 months in late 1991 to replace the older vessel of the same name.
Originally M/V POLAR CIRCLE, renamed HMS POLAR CIRCLE (A176) and then purchased by MOD(N) and renamed again in October 1992 to current name. Spends 4-6
months each year in the South Atlantic supporting the British Antarctic Survey. Will remain
in service until at least 2015.

Griffon 2000 TDX (M)

ROYAL MARINE CRAFT

4 GRIFFON 2000 TDX (M) LCAC

Pennants C21 - C24 **G.R.T.** 6.8 tons **Dimensions** 12m x 5m **Speed** 33 knots
Armament 1 x GPMG **Complement** 2

Notes
Ordered in April 1993, these four lightly armoured Landing Craft Air Cushion (LCAC) are operated by 539 Assault Squadron. Used extensively during the Iraq War to patrol the marshlands and waterways around Basra. They have the capacity to lift 12 fully equipped troops or 2 x 1000kg pallets of stores and are capable of deployment in C-130 Hercules transport aircraft. It is expected that the current fleet of hovercraft will be replaced in the short term.

SPECIALIST CRAFT

In addition to the familiar Rigid Raiding Craft and Rigid Inflatable Boats the Royal Marines have taken delivery of the Offshore Raiding Craft (ORC). It can be configured to transport up to eight fully-equipped commandos at speeds of over 35 knots. It can also be fitted with bullet-proof panels and weapon mountings to become a heavily-armed fire support vessel. Other vessels available include Air transportable Fast Insertion Craft (FIC) with a speed of 55 knots in addition to advanced wave piercing designs.

Swimmer Delivery Vehicles (SDV), in reality miniature submarines, which can be deployed from dry deck shelters on larger submarines, are also a part of the UK Special Forces inventory.

10 LCU Mk10

Pennants L1001 - L1010 **G.R.T.** 240 tons FL **Dimensions** 29.8m x 7.4m x 1.7m **Speed** 8.5 knots **Complement** 7.

Notes

Ro-Ro style landing craft designed to operate from the Albion class LPDs. Ordered in 1998 from Ailsa Troon. The first two were delivered in 1999. The remainder were built by BAE Systems at Govan. Capable of lifting one Main Battle Tank or four lighter vehicles. Capacity for 120 troops. Several older LCU Mk9s remain in service and saw service in Kuwait during the Iraq War.

23 LCVP Mk5

Pennants 9473, 9673-9692, 9707, 9708 **G.R.T.** 25 tons FL **Dimensions** 15m x 4m x 1.5m **Speed** 20 knots **Complement** 3.

Notes

First one ordered in 1995 from Vosper Thornycroft and handed over in 1996. A further four were delivered in December 1996 to operate from OCEAN, with two more for training at RM Poole ordered in 1998. A further 16 were ordered from Babcock in 2001. The Mk 5 can lift 8 tonnes of stores or a mix of 2 tonnes and 35 troops. These vessels have a greater range, lift and speed than the Mk 4s which they are gradually replacing.

ASTUTE

Ordered in 1997, the Astute class submarines were intended, initially, to replace the S class in RN service. The initial history of the programme was one of overspend and delays, leading in 2003 to a restructuring of the entire contract.

The programme now appears to be back on track with the first vessel, ASTUTE, scheduled to launch in June 2007, with delivery in August 2008 (planned In Service Date is January 2009). The other two submarines in the current order are AMBUSH and ARTFUL. The MoD and BAE are still agreeing a price for these boats and anticipate an order for Hull 04 in 2007. It has long been anticipated that a second batch would be ordered, for a class total of 8 submarines, but to date (November 2006) this has still not happened. To keep nuclear skills alive BAE have stated that an order every 22 months is essential to maintain a "drumbeat" of production. MoD have challenged BAE to cut the price of subsequent vessels by 30% for Hull 04 and 45% by Hull 06.

TYPE 45

The Type 45 Air Defence Destroyers are intended to replace the elderly Type 42s presently in service. Initially announced as a class of "up to" 12 ships, this was reduced in 2004 to just eight. Three ships, DARING, DIAMOND and DAUNTLESS are on firm order and under construction by BAE SYSTEMS on the Clyde and the VT Group at Portsmouth. A second batch of three, DEFENDER, DRAGON and DUNCAN have been announced but contract negotiations are still ongoing. There has been no breakthrough on negotiations for Hulls 07 and 08, indeed in some circles there have been reports of Government investigating what penalties there would be for terminating the contract at just five vessels. With the Equipment Plan budget under immense pressure, there is growing uncertainty over the ultimate number of ships that will eventually be acquired. The first of class, DARING, is scheduled to be delivered in September 2008.

FUTURE CARRIER PROGRAMME (CVF)

The CVF programme continues, but at a snail's pace. As expected France joined the programme in December 2005, so the expectation is that three ships will be built (two for RN, one for France). A main Gate submission was expected in October 2006 would lead to formal contracts for the construction the ships to be signed by the middle of 2007. There remain concerns that the budget for these 65,000 ton vessels is too tight and that ongoing negotiations over a "price gap" may have delayed the Main Gate decision. As we went to press (end November) there had been no formal announcement. The MoD have abandoned talk of an In-Service Date, stating that such a prediction cannot be made until contracts have been placed. Even assuming a 2007 order and 2008 start of construction, BAE have talked of a 2014 ISD as being extremely challenging, but achievable.

MILITARY AFLOAT REACH AND SUSTAINABILITY (MARS)

The future re-equipment of the RFA rests with this programme in which it is envisioned 11 ships will be procured (Five fleet tankers - delivered 2011 to 2015; Three joint sea-based logistics vessels - 2016, 2017 and 2020; Two fleet solid-support ships - 2017 and 2020 and a single fleet tanker - 2021). The main investment decision (Main Gate) is expected in September 2008, with the first ships expected to enter RFA service in 2012.

JOINT CASUALTY TREATMENT SHIP (JCTS)

Although the JCTS programme was "under review" In 2006, with the extension in service of RFA ARGUS to 2020 it is to all intents and purposes a project in abeyance. With the announcement of the MARS project it is quite possible that the JCTS requirement will be

THE ROYAL FLEET AUXILIARY

The Royal Fleet Auxiliary (RFA) is a civilian manned fleet, owned by the Ministry of Defence. Traditionally, its main task has been to replenish warships of the Royal Navy at sea with fuel, food, stores and ammunition to extend their operations away from base support. However, as the RN surface fleet has shrunk, the RFA has found itself fulfilling an operational role in addition to its support functions. Specialist ships provide aviation training; state of the art amphibious ships are arriving in the fleet; many of the ships can support and operate helicopters and several are equipped with hospital facilities.

There are 19 ships in the fleet; 8 Fleet and Support tankers, 2 Dry Cargo Fleet Replenishment Ships, 2 "one stop" replenishment ships, providing both dry stores and fuel, 4 Landing Ships Dock, 1 Landing Ships (Logistic), 1 Aviation Training Ship and 1 Forward Repair Ship.

The tanker fleet comprises two modern fleet tankers of the Wave class, together with six older single-hulled tankers (2 Rover Class and 4 Leaf Class) which are in urgent need of replacement. Over the past twelve months, a Wave class tanker has been on station in the Caribbean, with an embarked helicopter an RM detachment, operating on the frontline in the counter narcotics role - several high profile intercepts by WAVE RULER have highlighted the operational flexibility of these ships. The Fort Victoria class are also able to supply fuel while underway, as can the Aviation Support Ship ARGUS.

The old Knight class LSLs have all but disappeared from the fleet (the modernised SIR BEDIVERE being the sole survivor), being replaced by the larger and much more capable Bay class, the first of which, MOUNTS BAY, completed its first operational deployment in 2006 as part of Operation Vela.

The Repair Ship DILIGENCE returned to the UK at the end of 2006 after an absence of five years, during which time, she supported the fledgling Iraqi Navy in the Gulf and submarine operations from the Indian Ocean to the South Atlantic.

The focus for the future RFA is to see the Military Afloat Reach and Sustainability (MARS) programme through to service, potentially providing the RFA with a modern and flexible fleet combining both support functions and a warfighting capability.

While the RN continues a high operational tempo, with operational deployments in support of the Global War on Terror, in addition to its normal peacetime taking, the RFA will be there to provide support and as an operational "force multiplier" when required.

SHIPS OF THE ROYAL FLEET AUXILIARY
Pennant Numbers

Ship	Pennant Number	Ship	Pennant Number	Ship	Pennant Number
BRAMBLELEAF	A81	BLACK ROVER	A273	SIR BEDIVERE	L3004
BAYLEAF	A109	FORT ROSALIE	A385	LARGS BAY	L3006
ORANGELEAF	A110	FORT AUSTIN	A386	LYME BAY	L3007
OAKLEAF	A111	FORT VICTORIA	A387	MOUNTS BAY	L3008
DILIGENCE	A132	FORT GEORGE	A388	CARDIGAN BAY	L3009
ARGUS	A135	WAVE KNIGHT	A389		
GOLD ROVER	A271	WAVE RULER	A390		

KEEP UP TO DATE THROUGHOUT THE YEAR

Warship World is published six times a year (Jan, Mar, May, Jul, Sep, Nov) and gives you all the information necessary to keep this book updated throughout the year. Now in full colour.

This book is updated and re-issued every *December*. Keep up to date ... Don't miss the new edition.

Phone 01579 343663 or visit: www.navybooks.com

• NICK NEWNS

RFA Wave Ruler

FLEET TANKERS
WAVE CLASS

Ship	Pennant Number	Completion Date	Builder
WAVE KNIGHT	A 389	2002	BAE SYSTEMS
WAVE RULER	A 390	2002	BAE SYSTEMS

Displacement 31,500 tons (Full Load) **Dimensions** 196 x 27 x 10m **Speed** 18 knots
Armament 2 x Vulcan Phalanx (fitted for but not with), 2 x 30mm **Aircraft** 1 Merlin
Complement 80 (plus 22 Fleet Air Arm)

Notes

These 31,500-tonne ships are diesel-electric powered, with three refueling rigs, and aviation facilities to operate Merlin helicopters. They have a cargo capacity of 16,900 tonnes (Fuel) and 915 tonnes (Dry Stores).

• NICK NEWNS

RFA Oakleaf

SUPPORT TANKERS

Ship	Pennant Number	Completion Date	Builder
OAKLEAF	A111	1981	Uddevalla

Displacement 49,310 tons **Dimensions** 173.7m x 32.2m x 11.2m **Speed** 14 knots **Complement** 35.

Notes

At 49,310 tons displacement, she is the largest vessel in RN/RFA service. Her role, along with other support tankers, is to provide the fuel vital to enable the Navy's warships to operate far from their UK bases. Originally acquired on Bareboat charter, the ship was purchased by the MoD in September 2004. Decommissioning date has been brought forward from 2015 to 2010.

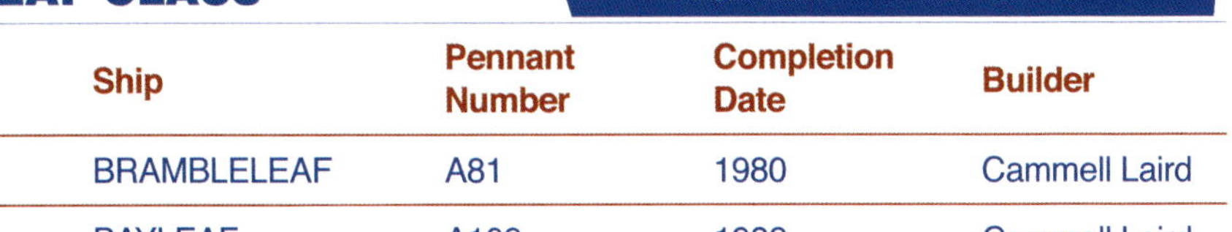

• NICK NEWNS **RFA Brambleleaf**

LEAF CLASS

Ship	Pennant Number	Completion Date	Builder
BRAMBLELEAF	A81	1980	Cammell Laird
BAYLEAF	A109	1982	Cammell Laird
ORANGELEAF	A110	1982	Cammell Laird

Displacement 37,747 tons **Dimensions** 170m x 26m x 12m **Speed** 14.5 knots **Complement** 60.

Notes

All are ex-merchant ships, originally acquired for employment mainly on freighting duties. All have been modified to enable them to refuel warships at sea. BRAMBLELEAF and BAYLEAF are now MoD(N) owned, with ORANGELEAF on long-term bareboat charter. All are commercial Stat32 class tankers. ORANGELEAF and BRAMBLELEAF are to decommission in 2009 and BAYLEAF in 2010.

The MoD also has also renewed the charter of the commercial tanker MAERSK RAPIER. She is a multi-tasked tanker which supplies fuel to the naval facilities in the UK, Gibraltar, the Falkland Islands and Souda Bay, Crete. She is also chartered to supply aviation fuel to Cyprus, Ascension Island and the Falkland Islands. The MoD charters the vessel to commercial companies when it is not in use for their own requirements.

• NICK NEWNS

RFA Gold Rover

ROVER CLASS

Ship	Pennant Number	Completion Date	Builder
GOLD ROVER	A271	1974	Swan Hunter
BLACK ROVER	A273	1974	Swan Hunter

Displacement 11,522 tons **Dimensions** 141m x 19m x 7m **Speed** 18 knots **Armament** 2 - 20mm guns **Complement** 49/54

Notes

Small Fleet Tankers designed to supply warships with fresh water, dry cargo and refrigerated provisions, as well as a range of fuels and lubricants. Helicopter deck, but no hangar. Have been employed in recent years mainly as support for HM Ships operating around the Falkland Islands and as the FOST station tanker. GREY ROVER decommissioned in 2006, to be followed by GOLD ROVER in 2009 and BLACK ROVER in 2010.

• CHRIS ROGERS

RFA Fort Rosalie

STORES VESSELS
FORT CLASS I

Ship	Pennant Number	Completion Date	Builder
FORT ROSALIE	A385	1978	Scott Lithgow
FORT AUSTIN	A386	1979	Scott Lithgow

Displacement 23,384 tons **Dimensions** 183m x 24m x 9m **Speed** 20 knots **Complement** 201, (120 RFA, 36 MoD Civilians & 45 Fleet Air Arm).

Notes

Full hangar and maintenance facilities are provided and up to four Sea King or RN Lynx helicopters can be carried for both the transfer of stores and anti-submarine protection of a group of ships (note: these ships are not cleared to operate Merlin). Both ships can be armed with 4 - 20mm guns. FORT ROSALIE is to decommission in 2013 and FORT AUSTIN in 2014.

RFA Fort Victoria

REPLENISHMENT SHIPS
FORT CLASS II

Ship	Pennant Number	Completion Date	Builder
FORT VICTORIA	A387	1992	Harland & Wolff
FORT GEORGE	A388	1993	Swan Hunter

Displacement 35,500 tons **Dimensions** 204m x 30m x 9m **Speed** 20 knots **Armament** 4 - 30mm guns, 2 x Phalanx CIWS, Sea Wolf Missile System (Fitted for but not with) **Complement** 100 (RFA), 24 MoD Civilians, 32 RN and up to 122 Fleet Air Arm.

Notes

"One stop" replenishment ships with the widest range of armaments, fuel and spares carried. Can operate up to 5 Sea King/Lynx or 3 Merlin Helicopters (more in a ferry role) with full maintenance facilities onboard. Medical facilities were upgraded with a 12 bed surgical capability. Both are to remain in service until 2019.

• NICK NEWNS

RFA Sir Bedivere

LANDING SHIPS (LOGISTIC)
SIR CLASS

Ship	Pennant Number	Completion Date	Builder
SIR BEDIVERE	L3004	1967	Hawthorn

Displacement 7,700 tons **Dimensions** 137m x 20m x 4m **Speed** 17 knots **Armament** Can be fitted with 20 or 40mm guns in emergency **Complement** 65

Notes

Manned by the RFA but tasked by the Commodore Amphibious Task Group (COMATG), this ship is used for heavy secure transport of stores – embarked by bow and stern doors. Can operate helicopters from both vehicle and flight decks if required and carry 340 troops. She completed a Ship Life Extension Programme (SLEP) at Rosyth in 1998. Occasionally used for MCMV support. SIR BEDIVERE is likely to continue in service until 2017. SIR GALAHAD and SIR TRISTRAM paid off in 2006 and are awaiting disposal. It is reported that both may find further service within the MoD, SIR TRISTRAM as a harbour training replacement for RAME HEAD and SIR GALAHAD as an accommodation ship to replace the former guided missile destroyer BRISTOL at Portsmouth.

• CHRIS ROGERS

RFA Largs Bay

LANDING SHIP DOCK (AUXILIARY)
BAY CLASS

Ship	Pennant Number	Completion Date	Builder
LARGS BAY	L3006	2006	Swan Hunter
LYME BAY	L3007	2007	Swan Hunter
MOUNTS BAY	L3008	2006	BAE SYSTEMS
CARDIGAN BAY	L3009	2007	BAE SYSTEMS

Displacement 16,190 tonnes **Dimensions** 176.6m x 26.4m x 5.1m **Speed** 18 knots
Armament Fitted to receive in emergency **Complement** 60

Notes

MOUNTS BAY entered operational service in September 2006. LYME BAY, the final ship of the class was towed from Swan Hunters in 2006 for completion by BAE Systems. The dock is capable of operating LCU 10s and they carry two LCVP Mk5s. They can offload at sea, over the horizon In addition to their war fighting role they could be well suited to disaster relief and other humanitarian missions. LARGS BAY entered service in December 2006; CARDIGAN BAY due to enter service in February 2007 and LYME BAY in November 2007.

RFA Diligence

FORWARD REPAIR SHIP

Ship	Pennant Number	Completion Date	Builder
DILIGENCE	A132	1981	Oesundsvarvet

Displacement 10,595 tons **Dimensions** 120m x 12m x 3m **Speed** 15 knots **Armament** 2 - 20mm **Complement** RFA 40, RN Personnel - approx 100.

Notes

Formerly the M/V Stena Inspector purchased (£25m) for service in the South Atlantic. Her deep diving complex was removed and workshops added. When not employed on "battle repair" duties can serve as support vessel for MCMVs and submarines on deployment. Scheduled to decommission in 2006, this date has now been extended to 2014. A probable replacement will be required, the likely earliest date for such being 2014. DILIGENCE returned to the UK at the end of 2006 after five years away.

• NICK NEWNS

RFA Argus

AVIATION TRAINING SHIP

Ship	Pennant Number	Completion Date	Builder
ARGUS	A135	1981	Cantieri Navali Breda

Displacement 28,481 tons (full load) **Dimensions** 175m x 30m x 8m **Speed** 18 knots
Armament 4 - 30 mm, 2 - 20 mm **Complement** 254 (inc 137 Fleet Air Arm)
Aircraft 6 Sea King/Merlin, 12 Harriers can be carried in a "ferry role".

Notes

Formerly the M/V CONTENDER BEZANT taken up from trade during the Falklands crisis. Purchased in 1984 (£13 million) for conversion to an 'Aviation Training Ship'. A £50 million re-build was undertaken at Belfast from 1984-87. Undertook rapid conversion in October 1990 to a Primary Casualty Reception Ship for service in the Gulf. These facilities were upgraded and made permanent during 2001. Originally scheduled to decommission in 2008, this date has now been extended to 2020. A replacement for the Aviation Ship and PCRS role is currently under review. A new RFA PCRS is almost certain, but probaly not in a dual role as an Aviation ship and PCRS. If a new purpose-built/adapted ship is not acquired a likely scenario is that other RFAs with deck/hangar facilities will be used for aviation training (as is the case now when ARGUS is unavailable) or the task may be carried out on RN ships with flight decks.

• NICK NEWNS　　　**MV Hurst Point**

STRATEGIC SEALIFT
RO-RO VESSELS

Ship	Pennant Number	Completion Date	Builder
HURST POINT		2002	Flensburger
HARTLAND POINT		2002	Harland & Wolff
EDDYSTONE		2002	Flensburger
LONGSTONE		2003	Flensburger
ANVIL POINT		2003	Harland & Wolff
BEACHY HEAD		2003	Flensburger

Displacement 10,000 tonnes, 13,300 tonnes (FL) **Dimensions** 193m x 26m x 6.6m
Speed 18 knots **Complement** 38

Notes
Foreland Shipping Limited (formerly AWSR) built 6 ro-ro vessels at yards in the UK and Germany under a PFI deal which was signed with the MoD on 27 June 2002 and runs until 31 December 2024. The Strategic Sealift Service requires Foreland to supply four vessels to the MoD on a full time basis with the other two vessels being available only to cover a limited number of pre-determined situations. The two vessels not employed by the MoD, BEACHY HEAD and LONGSTONE, are on charter to Transfennica, a Finnish subsidiary of the Spliethoff Group. The company itself and its six ships are all named after English light-houses. The ships come under the operational umbrella of Defence Supply Chain Operation and Movements (DSCOM), part of the Defence Logistics Organisation.

48

HMS ENTERPRISE
Dave Cullen

Dave Cullen
HMS OCEAN

HMS BULWARK
Nick Newns

HMS HURWORTH
Chris Rogers
M39

RFA BLACK ROVER
Nick Newns

RFA CARDIGAN BAY

Dave Cullen

HMS CAMPBELTOWN
Mike Welsford

HMS ARGYLL
Mike Palmer

MARINE SERVICES SUPPORT

The Defence Logistic Organisation (DLO) is tasked with Tri-Service provision of Marine Services and is responsible for In and Out-of-Port maritime services in support of Naval Bases, CinC Fleet, The Meteorological Office, QinetiQ (formerly DERA), RAF and Army. Their role is to undertake Mooring and Navigation buoy maintenance and maritime support to the underwater research programme. In port they undertake sea-borne services to the Fleet, including towage, passenger services, liquid delivery and receipt and sea-borne transfer of ammunition via barges.

Maritime services at the Kyle of Lochalsh are provided primarily to support the BUTEC Ranges, and secondarily to fulfil Fleet requirements in that area. In the three main ports at Portsmouth, Devonport and Clyde the service is currently delivered under a Government Owned/Commercially Operated (GOCO) contract with SERCo-Denholm Ltd. The vessels being operated on a BARECON (Bareboat charter) basis.

The current provision of marine service support is out for re-tender. The RMAS have been given the opportunity of bidding for a percentage of the work similar to that which they undertake at present. Within all solutions both the RMAS and industry are being offered all existing assets and have been encouraged to submit a vessel replacement programme.

For Mooring Maintenance, RMAS NEWTON and services at Kyle of Lochalsh, the service is currently delivered in house by the General Manager RMAS from his HQ at Pembroke Dock.

A 10-year PPP/PFI contract with an effective date of 1 April 2002 was placed with Smit International (Scotland) Ltd to carry out Marine Support to Ranges and Air Crew Training. Since that date Smit have replaced all the MoD craft with a fleet of new and second hand tonnage.

Marine Services vessels can be seen at work in the UK Naval Bases and are easily identified by their black hulls, buff coloured superstructure and by their Flag, which in the case of GM RMAS vessels, is a blue ensign defaced in the fly by a yellow anchor over two wavy lines. The remaining vessels fly the other Government ensign. Which is a blue ensign defaced in the fly by a yellow anchor.

SHIPS OF
THE MARINE SERVICES
Pennant Numbers

Ship	Pennant Number	Page	Ship	Pennant Number	Page
MELTON	A83	71	ADEPT	A224	60
MENAI	A84	71	BUSTLER	A225	60
MEON	A87	71	CAPABLE	A226	60
TORNADO	A140	74	CAREFUL	A227	60
TORMENTOR	A142	74	FAITHFUL	A228	60
WATERMAN	A146	73	COL. TEMPLER	A229	65
FRANCES	A147	63	DEXTEROUS	A231	60
FLORENCE	A149	63	ADAMANT	A232	70
GENEVIEVE	A150	63	SHEEPDOG	A250	61
KITTY	A170	62	NEWHAVEN	A280	67
LESLEY	A172	62	NUTBOURNE	A281	67
HUSKY	A178	61	NETLEY	A282	67
SALUKI	A182	61	OBAN	A283	68
SALMOOR	A185	75	ORONSAY	A284	68
SALMAID	A187	75	OMAGH	A285	68
BOVISAND	A191	66	PADSTOW	A286	69
CAWSAND	A192	66	IMPULSE	A344	59
HELEN	A198	63	IMPETUS	A345	59
MYRTLE	A199	62	NEWTON	A367	64
SPANIEL	A201	61	WARDEN	A368	77
FORCEFUL	A221	60	OILPRESS	Y21	72
NIMBLE	A222	60	MOORHEN	Y32	76
POWERFUL	A223	60	MOORFOWL	Y33	76

TUGS

IMPULSE CLASS

Ship	Pennant Number	Completion Date	Builder
IMPULSE	A344	1993	R. Dunston
IMPETUS	A345	1993	R. Dunston

G.R.T. 400 tons approx **Dimensions** 33m x 10m x 4m **Speed** 12 knots **Complement** 5.

Notes

Completed in 1993 specifically to serve as berthing tugs for the Trident Class submarines at Faslane. Both operated under contract by Serco Denholm.

MV Bustler

TWIN UNIT TRACTOR TUGS (TUTT'S)

Ship	Pennant Number	Completion Date	Builder
FORCEFUL	A221	1985	R. Dunston
NIMBLE	A222	1985	R. Dunston
POWERFUL	A223	1985	R. Dunston
ADEPT	A224	1980	R. Dunston
BUSTLER	A225	1981	R. Dunston
CAPABLE	A226	1981	R. Dunston
CAREFUL	A227	1982	R. Dunston
FAITHFUL	A228	1985	R. Dunston
DEXTEROUS	A231	1986	R. Dunston

G.R.T. 375 tons **Dimensions** 39m x 10m x 4m **Speed** 12 knots **Complement** 9.

Notes
The principal harbour tugs in naval service. All operated under contract by Serco Denholm except CAPABLE at Gibraltar which is managed locally.

• NICK NEWNS **MV Saluki**

DOG CLASS

Ship	Pennant Number	Completion Date	Builder
HUSKY	A178	1969	Appledore
SALUKI	A182	1969	Appledore
SPANIEL	A201	1967	Appledore
SHEEPDOG	A250	1969	Appledore

G.R.T. 152 tons **Dimensions** 29m x 8m x 4m **Speed** 12 knots **Complement** 5.

Notes

General harbour tugs – all completed between 1965 and 1969. COLLIE and CAIRN replaced at Kyle of Lochalsh by civilian vessels under charter to MoD during 2001. The tug MT ATLAS has been bareboat chartered by SERCo/Denholm at Portsmouth. SALUKI operates at Devonport, SHEEPDOG was scheduled to be withdrawn in 2005 but remains in service at Portsmouth. SPANIEL and HUSKY operate on the Clyde.

TRITON CLASS

Ship	Pennant Number	Completion Date	Builder
KITTY	A170	1972	R. Dunston
LESLEY	A172	1973	R. Dunston
MYRTLE	A199	1973	R. Dunston

G.R.T. 89 tons **Speed** 8 knots **Complement** 4.

Notes

Known as Water Tractors these craft are used for basin moves and towage of light barges. Operated by Serco Denholm Ltd. KITTY was proposed to be withdrawn from operations in 2003 but remains in service at Portsmouth. LESLEY and MYRTLE operate at Devonport.

• NICK NEWNS **MV Florence**

FELICITY CLASS

Ship	Pennant Number	Completion Date	Builder
FLORENCE	A149	1980	R. Dunston
FRANCES	A147	1980	R. Dunston
GENEVIEVE	A150	1980	R. Dunston
HELEN	A198	1974	R. Dunston

G.R.T. 80 tons **Speed** 10 knots **Complement** 4.

Notes

Water Tractors used for the movement of small barges and equipment. All are operated by Serco Denholm. Two sister vessels (GEORGINA and GWENDOLINE) sold to Serco Denholm in 1996 for service in H M Naval bases. FLORENCE and FRANCES operate at Devonport, GENEVIEVE and HELEN at Portsmouth.

RESEARCH VESSELS

Ship	Pennant Number	Completion Date	Builder
NEWTON	A367	1976	Scotts

G.R.T. 2,779 tons **Dimensions** 99m x 16m x 6m **Speed** 15 knots **Complement** 27

Notes

Primarily used in the support of RN training exercises. Some limited support provided for various trials. Operated by the RMAS. Completed major refit in 2001 to extend life. Is frequently seen with Royal Marine small craft embarked and is used as a training platform.

• DAVE CULLEN

MV Colonel Templer

Ship	Pennant Number	Completion Date	Builder
COLONEL TEMPLER	A 229	1966	Hall Russell

Displacement 1,300 tons **Dimensions** 56m x 11m x 5.6 m **Speed** 12 knots
Complement 14

Notes

Built as a stern trawler but converted in 1980 for use by the Defence Evaluation and
Research Agency as an acoustic research vessel. A major rebuild was completed after
a serious fire gutted the ship in 1990. 12 scientists can be carried. From Nov 2000 operated on the Clyde by Serco Denholm. Used in support of trials and converted in 2001 to
support RN diving training.

TENDERS
STORM CLASS

Ship	Pennant Number	Completion Date	Builder
BOVISAND	A191	1997	FBM (Cowes)
CAWSAND	A192	1997	FBM (Cowes)

G.R.T 225 tonnes **Dimensions** 23m x 11m x 2m **Speed** 15 knots **Complement** 5

Notes

These craft are used in support of Flag Officer Sea Training (FOST) at Plymouth to transfer staff quickly and comfortably to and from Warships and Auxiliaries within and beyond the Plymouth breakwater in open sea conditions. These are the first vessels of a small waterplane area twin hull (SWATH) design to be ordered by the Ministry of Defence and cost £6.5 million each. Speed restrictions implemented due to wash problems generated by these vessels.

• MICHAEL NITZ **MV Newhaven**

NEWHAVEN CLASS

Ship	Pennant Number	Completion Date	Builder
NEWHAVEN	A280	2000	Aluminium SB
NUTBOURNE	A281	2000	Aluminium SB
NETLEY	A282	2001	Aluminium SB

Tonnage 77 tonnes (45 grt) **Dimensions** 18.3m x 6.8m x 1.88m **Speed** 10 knots **Complement** 3 Crew (60 passengers).

Notes
MCA Class IV Passenger Vessels based at Portsmouth as replacements for Fleet tenders. Employed on general passenger duties within the port area.

• MIKE WELSFORD **MV Oban**

OBAN CLASS

Ship	Pennant Number	Completion Date	Builder
OBAN	A283	2000	McTay
ORONSAY	A284	2000	McTay
OMAGH	A285	2000	McTay

Tonnage 199 tons **Dimensions** 27.7m x 7.30m x 3.75m **Speed** 10 knots **Complement** 5 Crew (60 passengers).

Notes

MCA Class IIA Passenger Vessels which replaced Fleet tenders in 2001. OBAN was transferred to Devonport in 2003 for use in supporting passenger transfers and is occasionally used in support of FOST. ORONSAY and OMAGH employed on general passenger duties on the Clyde.

• CHRIS ROGERS **MV Padstow**

PADSTOW CLASS

Ship	Pennant Number	Completion Date	Builder
PADSTOW	A286	2000	Aluminium SB

Tonnage 77 tonnes (45 grt) **Dimensions** 18.3m x 6.8m x 1.88m **Speed** 10 knots **Complement** 3 Crew (60 passengers).

Notes
MCA Class VIA Passenger Vessel based at Plymouth. Used on general passenger ferrying duties and in support of FOST staff.

• DOUGLAS S. COULL   **MV Adamant**

PERSONNEL FERRY

Ship	Pennant Number	Completion Date	Builder
ADAMANT	A232	1992	FBM (Cowes)

G.R.T 170 tonnes **Dimensions** 30m x 8m x 1m **Speed** 22 knots **Complement** 5

Notes

Twin catamaran hulls based on the commercial Red Jet design (as used by Red Funnel Ferry Co). First water jet propulsion vessel owned by MoD(N). In service as a Clyde personnel ferry - operated by Serco Denholm.

FLEET TENDERS

Ship	Pennant Number	Completion Date	Builder
MELTON	A83	1981	Richard Dunston
MENAI	A84	1981	Richard Dunston
MEON	A87	1982	Richard Dunston

G.R.T. 78 tons **Dimensions** 24m x 6m x 3m **Speed** 10.5 knots **Complement** 4/5.

Notes

The last three survivors of a once numerous class of vessels used as Training Tenders, Passenger Ferries, or Cargo Vessels. MENAI and MEON are operated by Serco Denholm at Falmouth. MELTON is operated by the RMAS at Kyle. Expected to remain in service until the new contract for the Future Provision of Marine Services comes into service, an aspect of which will include a vessel replacement programme.

• DAVE CULLEN

MV Oilpress

COASTAL OILER

Ship	Pennant Number	Completion Date	Builder
OILPRESS	Y21	1969	Appledore Shipbuilders

G.R.T. 362 tons **Dimensions** 41m x 9m x 3m **Speed** 11 knots **Complement** 5.

Notes
Employed as Harbour and Coastal Oiler. Operated by Serco Denholm on the Clyde.

• DAVE CULLEN   MV Waterman

WATER CARRIER

Ship	Pennant Number	Completion Date	Builder
WATERMAN	A146	1978	R. Dunston

G.R.T. 263 tons **Dimensions** 40m x 8m x 2m **Speed** 11 knots **Complement** 5.

Notes
Capable of coastal passages, but normally supplies either demineralised or fresh water to the Fleet within port limits. WATERFOWL is owned and operated by Serco Denholm.

MV Tormentor

TORPEDO RECOVERY VESSELS (TRV) TORNADO CLASS

Ship	Pennant Number	Completion Date	Builder
TORNADO	A140	1979	Hall Russell
TORMENTOR	A142	1980	Hall Russell

G.R.T. 560 tons **Dimensions** 47m x 8m x 3m **Speed** 14 knots **Complement** 13.

Notes

All vessels have had suitable rails fitted to enable them to operate as exercise minelayers. Converted in 2002 to support RN diving training (in lieu of Fleet Tenders) in addition to their other roles. Both operate on the Clyde.

• DANIEL FERRO   **RMAS Salmoor**

MOORING & SALVAGE VESSELS
SAL CLASS

Ship	Pennant Number	Completion Date	Builder
SALMOOR	A185	1985	Hall Russell
SALMAID	A187	1986	Hall Russell

Displacement 2,200 tonnes   **Dimensions** 77m x 15m x 4m   **Speed** 15 knots
Complement 19

Notes
Multi-purpose vessels designed to lay and maintain underwater targets, navigation marks and moorings. SALMOOR is based at Greenock and SALMAID at Devonport. Both vessels can be deployed in support of submarine and submarine rescue operations.

• DAVID HANNAFORD

MV Moorfowl

MOOR CLASS

Ship	Pennant Number	Completion Date	Builder
MOORHEN	Y32	1989	McTay Marine
MOORFOWL	Y33	1989	McTay Marine

Displacement 518 tons **Dimensions** 32m x 11m x 2m **Speed** 8 knots **Complement** 10

Notes

Powered mooring lighters for use within sheltered coastal waters. Both operated by the RMAS in support of mooring maintenance. MOORHEN based at Portsmouth and MOORFOWL at Devonport. Both vessels also undertake coastal work.

TRIALS VESSEL

Ship	Pennant Number	Completion Date	Builder
WARDEN	A368	1989	Richards

Displacement 626 tons **Dimensions** 48m x 10m x 4m **Speed** 15 knots **Complement** 11.

Notes

Built as a Range Maintenance Vessel but now based at Kyle of Lochalsh and operated by the RMAS in support of BUTEC. Her earlier gantry has been removed and bridge structure extended aft. Also operates as a Remotely Operated Vehicle (ROV) platform. A replacement ROV has been installed and set to work to replace the older system.
The RMAS have taken two further trials craft on long term charter to help with the various tasks at the Kyle of Lochalsh. These are the SARA MAATJE VI on charter from Van Stee of Holland and LENIE on charter from Maritime Craft Services of Scotland.

Smit Dart

AIRCREW TRAINING VESSELS

Ship	Comp Date	Builder	Base Port
SMIT DEE	2003	BES Rosyth	Bukie
SMIT DART	2003	BES Rosyth	Plymouth
SMIT DON	2003	BES Rosyth	Blyth
SMIT YARE	2003	FBMA Cebu	Great Yarmouth
SMIT TOWY	2003	FBMA Cebu	Pembroke Dock
SMIT SPEY	2003	FBMA Cebu	Plymouth

G.R.T. 95.86 GRT **Dimensions** 27.6m x 6.6m x 1.5m **Speed** 21 knots **Complement** 6

Notes

The vessels were designed by FBM Babcock Marine and built in their shipyards in Scotland and the Philippines. Operated by SMIT International (Scotland) on behalf of the MoD for training military aircrew in marine survival techniques, helicopter winching drills and general marine support tasks. The design includes an aft docking well for a RIB or for torpedo recovery, a full width stern training platform and clear deck areas for helicopter winching drills. SMIT DART completed as a passenger vessel with larger superstructure. Two similar second-hand vessels, SMIT TAMAR and SMIT CYMRYAN are also employed in the same role. These vessels replaced the former RAF Spitfire class RTTLs in service.

RANGE SAFETY VESSELS

Ship	Comp Date	Builder
SMIT STOUR	2003	Maritime Partners Norway
SMIT ROTHER	2003	Maritime Partners Norway
SMIT ROMNEY	2003	Maritime Partners Norway
SMIT CERNE	2003	Maritime Partners Norway
SMIT FROME	2003	Maritime Partners Norway
SMIT MERRION	2003	Maritime Partners Norway
SMIT PENALLY	2003	Maritime Partners Norway
SMIT WAY	2003	Maritime Partners Norway
SMIT NEYLAND	2003	Maritime Partners Norway

G.R.T. 7.0 GRT **Dimensions** 12.3m x 2.83m x 0.89m **Speed** 35 knots **Complement** 2

Notes

A class of 12 metre Fast Patrol Craft which operate on Range Safety Duties at Dover, Portland and Pembroke. Have replaced the former RCT Sir and Honours class launches in this role.

• DANIEL FERRO

RCTV Arezzo

RAMPED CRAFT LOGISTIC

Vessel	Pennant Number	Completion Date	Builder
ARROMANCHES	L105	1987	James & Stone
ANDALSNES	L107	1984	James & Stone
AKYAB	L109	1984	James & Stone
AACHEN	L110	1986	James & Stone
AREZZO	L111	1986	James & Stone
AUDEMER	L113	1987	James & Stone

Displacement 165 tons **Dimensions** 33m x 8m x 1.5m **Speed** 9 knots
Complement 6.

Notes

Smaller - "all purpose" landing craft capable of carrying up to 96 tons. In service in coastal waters around Cyprus (ANDALSNES and AKYAB) and UK. ARROMANCHES was formerly AGHEILA (re-named 1994 when original vessel was sold). Several vessels sport green and black camouflage scheme.

British Aerospace HARRIER

Variants GR7, GR9, GR9A, T12.
Role Short take off, vertical landing (STOVL) strike, ground-attack and reconnaissance aircraft. T12 is two-seat trainer.
Engine 1 x Rolls Royce Pegasus 107 turbofan rated at 23,800lb thrust.
Span 30' 4"   **Length** 47' 1"   **Height** 11' 7"   **Max weight** 31,000lb.
Max speed 575 knots at low level.   **Crew** 1 pilot.
Avionics Hughes Angle Rate Bombing System (ARBS); thermal and infra-red imaging sensors; Zeus defensive aids suite including radar warning, ECM & chaff & flare dispensers; Night Vision Goggle (NVG) compatible cockpit.
Armament Up to 13,000lb of weapons on nine hard points. Inner wing stations can carry up to 2,000lb, outer wing stations intended only for Sidewinder missiles. Weapons include AGM 65 TV and IR guided air to surface missiles (ASM); Brimstone anti-armour ASM; Paveway II & III Laser Guided Bombs (LGB); CRV 7 rocket pods and up to 4 Sidewinder infra-red guided Air to Air Missiles (AAM). Inner wing stations carry 100 or 190 gallon drop tanks. A reconnaissance pod can be carried on the fuselage centre station.
Squadron service 800, 801 Squadrons.

Notes Both RN squadrons have a nominal complement of 9 Harriers and form part of Joint Force Harrier with 1 and 4 Squadrons of the RAF, shore based at RAF Cottesmore. 20 (Reserve) squadron at RAF Wittering trains both RN and RAF air and ground crews. All four front line units are available for use embarked in tailored air groups with the RN units spending proportionally more time at sea. The GR 9 has the up rated Pegasus 107 engine; the 9A will, in addition, have an open-architecture computer system for targeting and weapons management.

European Helicopter Industries EH101 MERLIN

Variants HM1
Role Anti-submarine and Maritime patrol
Engine 3 x Rolls-Royce Turbomeca RTM322 turboshafts each developing 2,100 shp
Length 74' 10" **Width** 14' 10" **Height** 21' 10" **Main Rotor Diameter** 61'
Max Weight 32,120 lbs
Max Speed 167 kts   **Range** 625 nm
Crew 3 (Pilot, Observer and Aircrewman)
Avionics Blue Kestrel 360 degree search radar, Orange Reaper ESM, passive and active sonar systems and AQS903 digital processor.
Armament 4 lightweight torpedoes or depth charges.
Squadron service 700M (OEU), 814, 820, 824, 829 Squadrons

Notes Developed by Agusta and Westland, as a consortium originally known as European Helicopter Industries, the Merlin is an advanced anti-submarine helicopter that can also be used for surface surveillance. Surprisingly, unlike the Italian version, the HM 1 cannot carry a weapon capable of attacking surface warships, limiting its usefulness in the contemporary battle space. 829 is the parent unit for up to 12 detachments planned to operate from Type 23 frigates. Other squadrons operate from RFAs and as part of carrier TAGs. A major upgrade programme costing £750 million was announced in 2006.

Agusta-Westland SEA KING

The basic Sea King airframe continues in RN service in a number of different roles. The following details are common to all.

Engines 2 x 1600shp Rolls Royce Gnome H 1400 – 1 free power turbines.
Rotor Diameter 62' 0" **Length** 54' 9" **Height** 17' 2" **Max Weight** 21,400lb
Max Speed 125 knots.

• NICK NEWNS

HAR 5 / 6

Roles Utility; COD (Carrier Onboard Delivery); SAR.
Crew 2 pilots, 1 observer and 1 aircrewman.
Avionics Sea Searcher radar; Orange Crop passive ESM equipment.
Armament A 7.62mm machine gun can be mounted in the doorway.
Squadron Service 771 NAS
Notes The HAR 5 continues to provide SAR coverage from Culdrose in the South West and from Prestwick in Scotland. Detachments are embarked in carriers and RFAs for combat SAR and COD duties.

ASaC 7

Role Airborne Surveilance and Control. **Crew:** 1 pilot and 2 observers.
Avionics Upgraded Thales Searchwater radar, Orange Crop passive ESM, Enhanced Communications System, Joint Tactical Information Distribution System (Link 16)
Squadron Service 849 HQ, 849A and 849B Flights in commission.

Notes
Used primarily for the airborne surveillance and control of the airspace over a maritime force the sensors can also 'see' and track targets on the sea surface and on land in the littoral battle space making the ASaC 7 an invaluable asset. The flights are, in reality, autonomous squadrons, two of which are available to form part of embarked TAGs at any one time. 15 Sea Kings have been converted to this role, 2 of which were lost in the Gulf in 2003.

• NICK NEWNS

HC 4, Mk6 (CR)

Role Commando assault and utility transport.
Crew 2 pilots and 1 aircrewman.   **Armament** Door mounted 7.62mm machine gun.
Squadron Service 845, 846 and 848 Squadrons.
Notes The HC4 has a fixed undercarriage with no sponsons or radome. It is equipped to carry up to 17 troops in the cabin or underslung loads of up to 6000 lbs. The three Commando Support squadrons are based at Yeovilton but (together with 847 NAS with its Army-type Lynx aircaft) form part of the Joint Helicopter Command (JHC) based at Wilton, a tri-Service formation whose purpose is to maximise the effectiveness of all battlefield helicopters. The Commando Support squadrons train to operate in all environments, from arctic to tropical, and can embark or detach at short notice to support 3 Commando Brigade or as required by the JHC. The HC4 has extensive armour plating and a sophisticated defensive aids suite. Some HAS 6 airframes, stripped of their radar and sonar and designated Mk 6 (CR) are used by Commando squadrons while HC 4s go through a refurbishment programme. In the new role, their undercarriages are locked in the 'down' position, like the HC 4.

• NICK NEWNS

• NICK NEWNS   **Lynx HAS8**

Agusta-Westland LYNX

Variants HAS 3, HMA 8, AH 7.
Roles Surface search and attack; anti-submarine attack; SAR; troop carrying.
Engines 2 x 900hp Rolls Royce GEM BS 360-07-26 free shaft turbines.
Rotor diameter 42' 0" **Length** 39' 1" **Height** 11' 0" **Max Weight** 9,500lb.
Max Speed 150 knots. **Crew** 1 pilot and 1 observer.
Avionics SEA SPRAY radar. Orange Crop passive ESM equipment. Sea Owl Passive Infrared Device (Mk 8).
Armament External pylons carry up to 4 - SEA SKUA air to surface missiles or 2 x STINGRAY torpedoes, depth charges and markers. 1 door mounted M3M 0.5" machine gun. Standard configuration for board and search operations now 1 x door mounted M3M, 1 x pylon mounted Sea Skua and rope for "rapid-roping" deployment of troops.
Squadron Service 702, 815 and 847 squadrons in commission.

Notes Lynx OEU (Operational Evaluation Unit) develops operational tactics for HMA 8 aircraft. 702 NAS is the training squadron. 815 squadron is the parent unit for single air-craft ships flights. Both squadrons are based at Yeovilton. Ships' Flights are divided approximately equally between HAS 3 and HMA 8 aircraft. Another version of the Lynx, the AH7, is operated by 847 NAS in a Commando Support role. There are 35 airframes each of the HMA8 and HAS3 versions. 30 new Lynx, with an option on 5 more, to an improved design have been ordered. These are expected to enter front-line service from 2015 by which time the older versions will have been withdrawn from service.

ILLUSTRIOUS, ARK ROYAL and OCEAN embark Tailored Air Groups (TAG) chosen to fulfil the specific mission for which the ship in question has been deployed. In the first two ships, 3 separate types can be embarked concurrently, selected from Harrier, Merlin, Sea King, Chinook and Apache squadrons. The Sea Kings are usually ASaC 7s but HC 4 and HAR 5 utility version can and do embark. OCEAN cannot support fixed-wing aircraft operationally although they can land, refuel and launch from her deck. TAGs embark with appropriate force commanders, responsible to PJHQ Northwood for the tactical employment of their aircraft and to their own Joint Force HQ for their operational readiness. Typically, a strike TAG has an RN captain or RAF group captain as force commander. A battlefield helicopter TAG could have either of these or an Army colonel. This operational structure has set in place the concepts that the MOD intends to use in the CVF when it joins the fleet. It is a doctrine unique to the UK armed forces.

● NICK NEWNS

Westland APACHE AH1

Variants AH 1
Role Attack and reconnaissance helicopter.
Engines 2 x Rolls Royce/Turbomeca RTM 322 turboshafts.
Rotor Diameter 17' 2" **Length** 58' 3" **Height** 15' 3" **Max Weight** 15,075lb.
Max Speed 150 knots   **Crew:** 2 pilots
Avionics Helicopter integrated defensive Aids Suite (HIDAS); Longbow radar, optical and infra-red target acquisition sensors.
Armament Up to 16 AGM 114 Hellfire anti-tank guided weapons; up to 4 Sidewinder air-to-air missiles; M230 30mm cannon with 1,160 rounds (chain gun); up to 76 CRV 7 unguided rockets.

Squadron Service 656 Squadron, 9 Regiment AAC allocated for maritime tasking.
Notes Army Air Corps Apaches have been cleared for embarked operations. With other joint assets they can form part of Tailored Air Groups (TAG) embarked for specific operational and training missions.

Boeing CHINOOK HC2

Variants HC 2
Role Battlefield transport helicopter.
Engines 2 x 3,750 shp Avco Lycoming T55-L-712 turboshafts.
Rotor Diameter 60' 0" **Length** 98' 9" **Height** 18' 8" **Max Weight** 50,000lb
Max Speed 160 knots   **Crew** 2 pilots, 1 aircrewman.
Avionics Infra-red jammer; chaff & flare dispenser, missile warning system.
Armament Up to 2 x M 134 miniguns and 1 x M 60 machine gun.
Squadron Service 18 Squadron RAF is declared in the maritime role.
Notes RAF Chinook squadrons form part of the Joint Helicopter Force with the RN commando squadrons. 18 Squadron aircraft embarked in ARK ROYAL during Operation Telic in 2003 and are frequently used to provide heavy lift during amphibious expeditionary operations. They are too large to strike down into the hangars in OCEAN, ILLUSTRIOUS and ARK ROYAL and have to have their rotor blades manually removed for parking on deck as they lack a conventional blade fold mechanism. The new CVF is being designed with Chinook operations in mind.

FLEET TARGET GROUP

792 Naval Air Squadron was commissioned at RNAS Culdrose in November 2001, from the Fleet Target Group which had transferred its operations from RNAS Portland on its closure in 1998.

The Squadron operates Mirach 100/5 unmanned high subsonic drones used to test the Sea Dart Missile System fitted to Type 42 Destroyers. They are also used to test Sidewinder missiles on Harriers and RAF Tornados. Meteor SPA of Italy builds the MIRACH 100/5 and 37 were ordered for 792 NAS. Take off is assisted by two rockets that fall away once the drone is airborne. The drone can be controlled by a ship or shore based operator.

The Italian company, Galileo Avionica, supplies the MIRACH 100/5 naval variant to the UK. In 2003 it signed a major contract with QinetiQ, the UK company responsible for British firing range operations. In this case, the MIRACH 100/5 was selected under the Replacement Aerial Target System (RATS) program to replace the British Jindivik aerial target previously used at the Aberporth range.

The MIRACH 100/5 can be launched from the flight deck of a Type 42, Fort or Rover Class RFAs, and is also launched from a land based site operated by QinetiQ at Aberporth in Wales. Once the MIRACH has completed its mission, it parachutes down into the sea to be recovered by helicopter and used again. An RAF Nimrod is always present while the drone is flying to ensure the range is clear at all times.

• NICK NEWNS

British Aerospace HAWK

Engine 1 x Adour Mk 151 5200 lbs thrust.
Crew 1 or 2 Pilots (both service and civilian)
Notes Used by Fleet Requirements and Aircraft Direction Unit (FRADU) at Culdrose to provide support for training of RN ships, RN Flying Standards Flight and as airborne targets for the Aircraft Direction School. The aircraft are operated by Babcock.

• NICK NEWNS

British Aerospace JETSTREAM T2 and T3

Engines 2 x 940hp Turbomeca Astazou 16D turboprops. (T3 Garrett turboprops).
Crew 1 or 2 pilots, 2 student observers plus 3 other seats.
Notes T2's are used by 750 Squadron at Culdrose for training Fleet Air Arm Observers. T3's are used by the 750 Heron detachment at Yeovilton for operational support/communications flying.

● LEE HOWARD

Aerospatiale AS365N DAUPHIN 2

Engines 2 x Turbomeca Arriel 1C1.
Crew 1 or 2 pilots.
Notes Operated by British International from Plymouth City Airport under MoD COMR (Civil Owned Military Registered) contract. Used to transfer Sea Training staff from shore and between ships operating in the Plymouth sea training areas during work-ups. Aircraft are also used for Guided Weapons System Calibration and Naval Gunfire Support.

● LEE HOWARD

GROB G115 D-2

Used for the flying grading of new entry aircrew and other light, fixed-wing tasks. They are civilian manned but operated on behalf of 727 squadron at Roborough near Plymouth. The squadron is due to move to RNAS Yeovilton.

Royal Navy Historic Flight

The RNHF is supported financially by the Swordfish Heritage Trust. The Historic Flight has been civilianised since 1993. The current (2006) holding of aircraft is:

Flying: 1 Sea Hawk, 1 Sea Fury.
Under Repair: 3 Fairey Swordfish.

• NICK NEWNS

Royal Navy Historic Flight Sea Fury

• NICK NEWNS

Royal Navy Historic Flight Seahawk

WEAPONS OF THE ROYAL NAVY

Sea Launched Missiles

Trident II D5

The American built Lockheed Martin Trident 2 (D5) submarine launched strategic missiles are Britain's only nuclear weapons and form the UK contribution to the NATO strategic deterrent. 16 missiles, each capable of carrying up to 6 UK manufactured thermonuclear warheads (but currently limited to 4 under current government policy), are aboard each of the Vanguard class SSBNs. Trident has a maximum range of 12,000 km and is powered by a three stage rocket motor. Launch weight is 60 tonnes, overall length and width are 13.4 metres and 2.1 metres respectively.

Tomahawk (BGM-109)

This is a land attack cruise missile with a range of 1600 km and can be launched from a variety of platforms including surface ships and submarines. Some 65 of the latter version were purchased from America to arm Trafalgar class SSNs with the first being delivered to the Royal Navy for trials during 1998. Tomahawk is fired in a disposal container from the submarine's conventional torpedo tubes and is then accelerated to its subsonic cruising speed by a booster rocket motor before a lightweight F-107 turbojet takes over for the cruise. Its extremely accurate guidance system means that small targets can be hit with precision at maximum range, as was dramatically illustrated in the Gulf War and Afghanistan. Total weight of the submarine version, including its launch capsule is 1816 kg, it carries a 450 kg warhead, length is 6.4 metres and wingspan (fully extended) 2.54 m. Fitted in T class submarines.

Harpoon

The Harpoon is a sophisticated anti-ship missile using a combination of inertial guidance and active radar homing to attack targets out to a range of 130 km, cruising at Mach 0.9 and carrying a 227 kg warhead. Fitted to the Batch II Type 22 and Type 23 frigates. It is powered by a lightweight turbojet but is accelerated at launch by a booster rocket. The RN also deploys the UGM-84 submarine launched version aboard its Swiftsure and Trafalgar class SSNs.

Sea Dart

A medium range area defence anti aircraft missile powered by a ramjet and solid fuel booster rocket. Maximum effective range is in the order of 80 km and the missile accelerates to a speed of Mach 3.5. It forms the main armament of the Type 42 destroyers. Missile weight 550 kg, length 4.4 m, wingspan 0.91 m.

Sea Wolf

Short range rapid reaction anti-missile missile and anti-aircraft weapon. The complete weapon system, including radars and fire control computers, is entirely automatic in operation. Type 22 frigates carry two sextuple Sea Wolf launchers but the subsequent Type 23 frigates carry 32 Vertical Launch Seawolf (VLS) in a silo on the foredeck. Basic missile data: weight 82 kg, length 1.9 m, wingspan 56 cm, range c.56 km, warhead 13.4 kg. The VLS missile is basically similar but has jettisonable tandem boost rocket motors.

Air Launched Missiles

Sea Skua

A small anti-ship missile developed by British Aerospace arming the Lynx helicopters carried by various frigates and destroyers. The missile weighs 147 kg, has a length of 2.85 m and a span of 62 cm. Powered by solid fuel booster and sustainer rocket motors, it has a range of over 15 km at high subsonic speed. Sea Skua is particularly effective against patrol vessels and fast attack craft, as was demonstrated in both the Falklands and Gulf Wars.

Sidewinder

This is one of the world's most successful short range air to air missiles. The latest AIM-9L version carried by Harriers uses a heat seeking infra red guidance system and has a range of 18 km. Powered by a solid fuel rocket motor boosting it to speeds of Mach 2.5, it weighs 86.6 kg and is 2.87 m long

Guns

114mm Vickers Mk8

The Royal Navy's standard medium calibre general purpose gun which arms the later Type 22s, Type 23 frigates and Type 42 destroyers. A new electrically operated version, the Mod 1, recognised by its angular turret, was introduced in 2001 and will be fitted in the Type 23, Type 22, some Type 42 and the Type 45 classes. Rate of fire: 25 rounds/min. Range: 22,000 m. Weight of Shell: 21 kg.

Goalkeeper

A highly effective automatic Close in Weapons System (CIWS) designed to shoot down missiles and aircraft which have evaded the outer layers of a ships defences. The complete system, designed and built in Holland, is on an autonomous mounting and includes radars, fire control computers and a 7-barrel 30 mm Gatling gun firing 4200 rounds/min. Goalkeeper is designed to engage targets between 350 and 1500 metres away.

Phalanx

A US built CIWS designed around the Vulcan 20 mm rotary cannon. Rate of fire is 3000 rounds/min and effective range is c.1500 m. Fitted in Type 42 destroyers, ARK ROYAL, OCEAN and the Fort Victoria class.

DS30B 30mm

Single 30mm mounting carrying an Oerlikon 30mm gun. Fitted to Type 23 frigates and various patrol vessels and MCMVs. In August 2005 it was announced that the DS30B fitted in Type 23 frigates was to be upgraded to DS30M Mk 2 to include new direct-drive digital servos and the replacement of the earlier Oerlikon KCB cannon with the ATK Mk 44 Bushmaster II 30 mm gun. Consideration is already being given to purchasing additional DS30M Mk 2 systems for minor war vessels and auxiliaries.

GAM BO 20mm

A simple hand operated mounting carrying a single Oerlikon KAA 200 automatic cannon firing 1000 rounds/min. Maximum range is 2000 m. Carried by most of the fleet's major warships except the Type 23 frigates.

20mm Mk.7A

The design of this simple but reliable weapon dates back to World War II but it still provides a useful increase in firepower, particularly for auxiliary vessels and RFAs. Rate of fire 500-800 rounds/min.

Close Range Weapons

In addition to the major weapons systems, all RN ships carry a variety of smaller calibre weapons to provide protection against emerging terrorist threats in port and on the high seas such as small fast suicide craft. In addition it is sometimes preferable, during policing or stop and search operations to have a smaller calibre weapon available. Depending upon the operational environment ships may be seen armed with varying numbers of pedestal mounted General Purpose Machine Guns (GPMG).   Another addition to the close in weapons is the Mk 44 Mini Gun a total of 150 of which have been procured from the United States as a fleetwide fit. Fitted to a naval post mount, the Minigun is able to fire up to 3,000 rounds per minute, and is fully self-contained (operating off battery power).

Torpedoes

Stingray

A lightweight anti submarine torpedo which can be launched from ships, helicopters or aircraft. In effect it is an undersea guided missile with a range of 11 km at 45 knots or 7.5 km at 60 knots. Length 2.1 m, diameter 330 mm. Aboard Type 42s and Type 22s Stingray is fired from triple tubes forming part of the Ships Torpedo Weapon System (STWS) but the newer Type 23s have the Magazine Torpedo Launch System (MTLS) with internal launch tubes. Sting Ray Mod 1 is intended to prosecute the same threats as the original Sting Ray but with an enhanced capability against small conventionally powered submarines and an improved shallow-water performance.

Spearfish

Spearfish is a submarine-launched heavyweight torpedo which has replaced Tigerfish. Claimed by the manufacturers to be the world's fastest torpedo, capable of over 70 kts, its sophisticated guidance system includes an onboard acoustic processing suite and tactical computer backed up by a command and control wire link to the parent submarine. Over 20ft in length and weighing nearly two tons, Spearfish is fired from the standard 21-inch submarine torpedo tube and utilises an advanced bi-propellant gas turbine engine for higher performance.

At the end of the line ...

Readers may well find other warships afloat which are not mentioned in this book. The majority have fulfilled a long and useful life and are now relegated to non-seagoing duties. The following list gives details of their current duties:

Pennant No	Ship	Remarks
	BRITANNIA	Ex Royal Yacht at Leith. Open to the public.
	CAROLINE	RNR Drill Ship at Belfast, Northern Ireland.
A134	RAME HEAD	Escort Maintenance Vessel - Royal Marines Training Ship in Fareham Creek (Portsmouth)
C35	BELFAST	World War II Cruiser Museum ship - Pool of London. Open to the public daily . Tel: 020 7940 6300
D23	BRISTOL	Type 82 Destroyer - Sea Cadet Training Ship at Portsmouth.
D73 S17	CAVALIER OCELOT	World War II Destroyer & Oberon class Submarine Museum Ships at Chatham. Partially open to the public. Tel: 01634 823800
F126 S21 M1115	PLYMOUTH ONYX BRONINGTON	With the collapse of the Warship Preservation Trust, the ships at Birkenhead, Wirral are closed to the public. ONYX has been moved to Barrow as part of the Dock Museum. PLYMOUTH and BRONINGTON remain at Birkenhead whilst discussions over their future placement continue.
S67	ALLIANCE	Submarine - Museum Ship at Gosport Open to the public daily. Tel: 023 92 511349
M1151 M1154	IVESTON KELLINGTON	(Thurrock) } Static Sea Cadet (Stockton upon Tees) } Training Vessels

At the time of publishing (December 2006) the following ships were laid up in long term storage or awaiting sale.

PORTSMOUTH: Intrepid; Fearless; Newcastle; Glasgow; Cardiff; Brecon; Cottesmore; Dulverton; Leeds Castle.

PLYMOUTH: Splendid, Spartan, Sovereign, Courageous; Conqueror; Valiant; Warspite.

ROSYTH: Resolution; Renown; Repulse; Revenge; Swiftsure; Churchill; Dreadnought.